Contents

T0386019

Welcome

1 ✏️ **Match and trace.**

① ② ③ ④

ⓐ Hello. I'm
Rita .

ⓑ Hello. I'm
Zak .

ⓒ Hello. My name's
Oscar .

ⓓ Hello. My name's
Millie .

2 **Trace. Then colour.**

(1) blue

(2) red

(3) yellow

(4) green

3 **Listen and tick (✓). Then colour.**

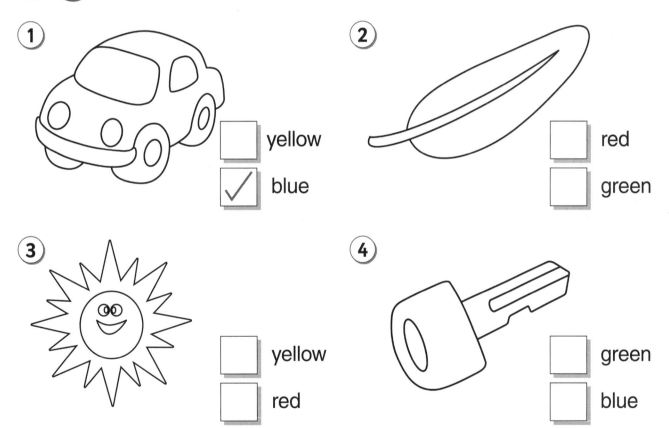

(1)
- [ ] yellow
- [✓] blue

(2)
- [ ] red
- [ ] green

(3)
- [ ] yellow
- [ ] red

(4)
- [ ] green
- [ ] blue

4 🖊️ **Read and trace.**

a 1 one
b 2 two
c 3 three
d 4 four
e 5 five

f 6 six
g 7 seven
h 8 eight
i 9 nine
j 10 ten

5 🖊️ **Count and trace.**

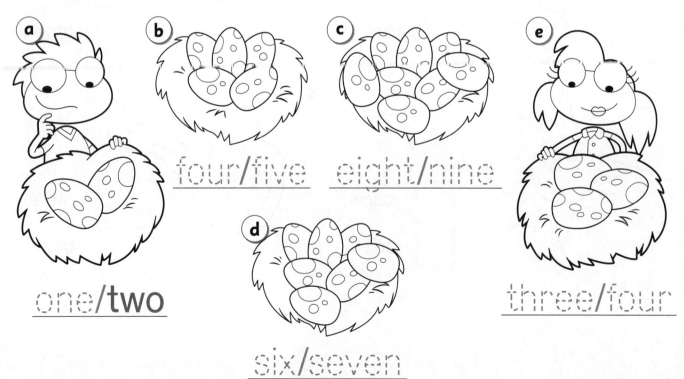

a one/two

b four/five

c eight/nine

d six/seven

e three/four

6 **Colour in. Then match and trace.**

①

②

③

④

ⓐ <u>Her</u>

ⓑ Her name's Millie.

ⓒ His name's Zak.

ⓓ His name's Oscar.

name's Rita.

 7 **Read and colour.**

①

②

His backpack is blue.   Her backpack is red.

8 (1:12) **Listen and number. Then write.**

sit down

9 ✏️ **Follow and colour.**

1

2

3

4

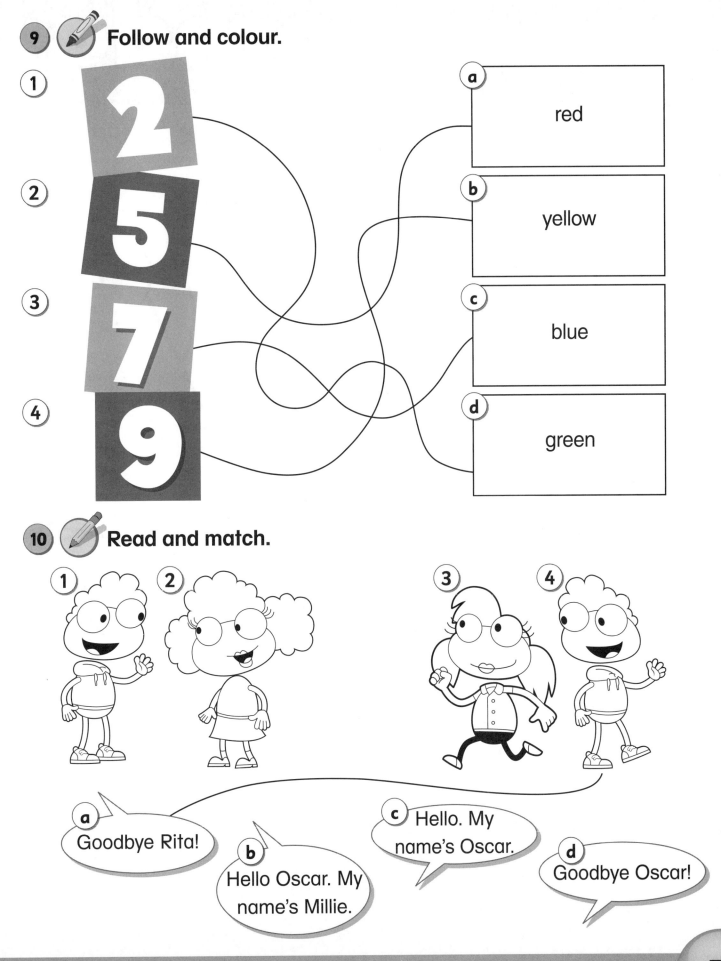

a red

b yellow

c blue

d green

10 ✏️ **Read and match.**

1 2   3 4

a Goodbye Rita!

b Hello Oscar. My name's Millie.

c Hello. My name's Oscar.

d Goodbye Oscar!

1 My birthday

1  **Trace and colour.**

1 pink

2 orange

3 black

4 brown

5 purple

6 white

Lesson 1 vocabulary (colours)

2 **Listen and number.**

a

b

c Ann | 1 |

3  **Look and trace. Then colour.**

a **I'm** ___four___. **My favourite colour is** **orange**.

b **I'm** ___seven___. **My favourite colour is** ___blue___.

c **I'm** ___nine___. **My favourite colour is** ___pink___.

d **I'm** ___ten___. **My favourite colour is** ___purple___.

Lesson 2 grammar (What's your name? How old are you? What's your favourite colour?)

④ ✏ Match. Then trace.

1

2

3

4

5

6

7

8

a   stamp

b   climb

c   run

d   jump

e   dance

f   clap

g   hop

h   walk

5 Read and trace. Then colour.

1

What colour is it?

It's <u>purple</u>.

2

What colour is it?

It's orange.

3

What colour is it ?

It's blue.

4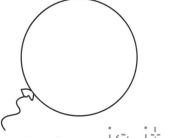

What colour is it?

It's yellow.

5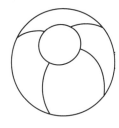

Is it red?

No , it isn't. It's pink.

6

Is it brown?

Yes , it is.

7

Is it white?

No, it isn't. It's green.

8

Is it black?

Yes, it is .

Lesson 4 grammar (*Is it purple? Yes, it is. / No, it isn't. What colour is it? It's blue.*)

6  **Read and circle. Then draw and colour.** STORY

1 Two green cakes for (Oscar) / Zak.

2 Two purple cakes for Rita / Millie.

3 Two orange cakes for Zak / Millie.

4 Two pink cakes for Oscar / Rita.

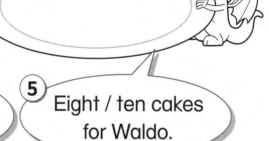

5 Eight / ten cakes for Waldo.

 7 **Look and write (✓) or (✗) .**

8 Read the words and circle.

pat   tap

PHONICS
a   p   s   t

9 🔊 1:26 Listen to the sounds and circle the letters.

1   t (p) a s

2   p s t a

3   s t p a

4   t a s p

10 🔊 1:27 Listen and write the letters.

1 t   2 ____   3 ____   4 ____

11 🔊 1:28 Listen and write the words.

1 s a t   2 ____   3 ____   4 ____

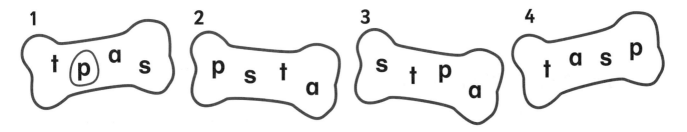

12 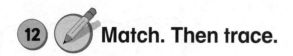 **Match. Then trace.**

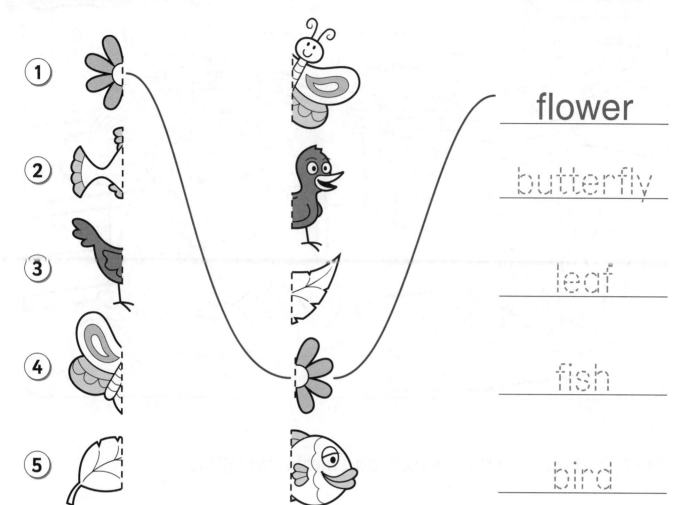

flower

butterfly

leaf

fish

bird

13  **Colour. Then circle.**

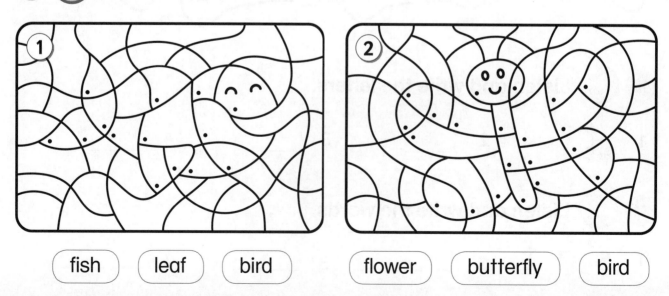

fish   leaf   bird   flower   butterfly   bird

Wider World

14 Trace and match.

1 birthday cake

2 birthday card

3 balloon

4 present

a

b

c

d

15 Draw and colour. Then write.

1 How old are you? _____

2 How many balloons? _____

3 What colour is the present? _____

Unit Review

16 Read and colour.

1	black
2	brown
3	blue
4	purple
5	pink
6	orange
7	green

17 Look and circle.

1 What's your name?   My name's Zak. / Her name's Zak.

2 How old are you?   It's six. / I'm six.

3 What's your favourite colour?   My favourite colour is blue. / His favourite colour is blue.

About Me

 18 **Read and write. Then colour.**

pink	~~My~~	is	I'm

Hello. ¹_____My_____ name's Ana.

² _____ seven.

My favourite colour

³ _____ pink.

Look! A ⁴ _____ butterfly!

Goodbye!

19 **Draw and write.**

Hello. My name's

_____.

I'm _____.

My favourite colour is

_____.

Goodbye!

2 At school

1 🖊 **Draw. Then trace.**

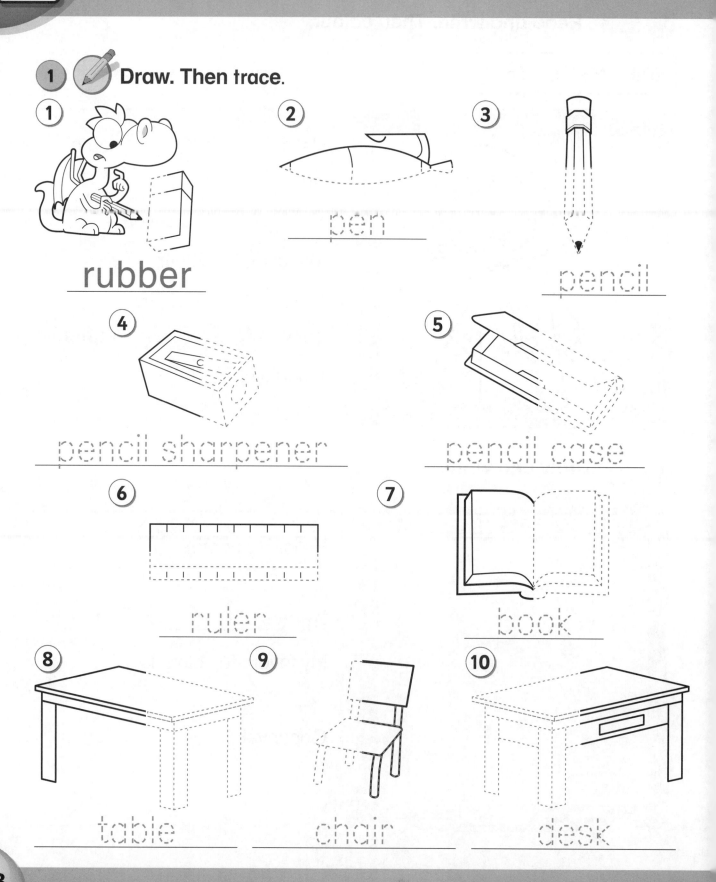

1 rubber

2 pen

3 pencil

4 pencil sharpener

5 pencil case

6 ruler

7 book

8 table

9 chair

10 desk

2 🖊️ **Read and match. Then colour.**

(1) It's a pencil sharpener. It's green.

(2) It's a table. It's brown.

(3) It's a chair. It's orange.

(4) It's a rubber. It's red and blue.

a

b

c

d

3 💿 1:38 **Listen, circle and tick (✓).**

(1) (black) / blue

☐   ✓

(2) pink / brown

☐   ☐

(3) purple / green

☐   ☐

(4) red / yellow

☐   ☐

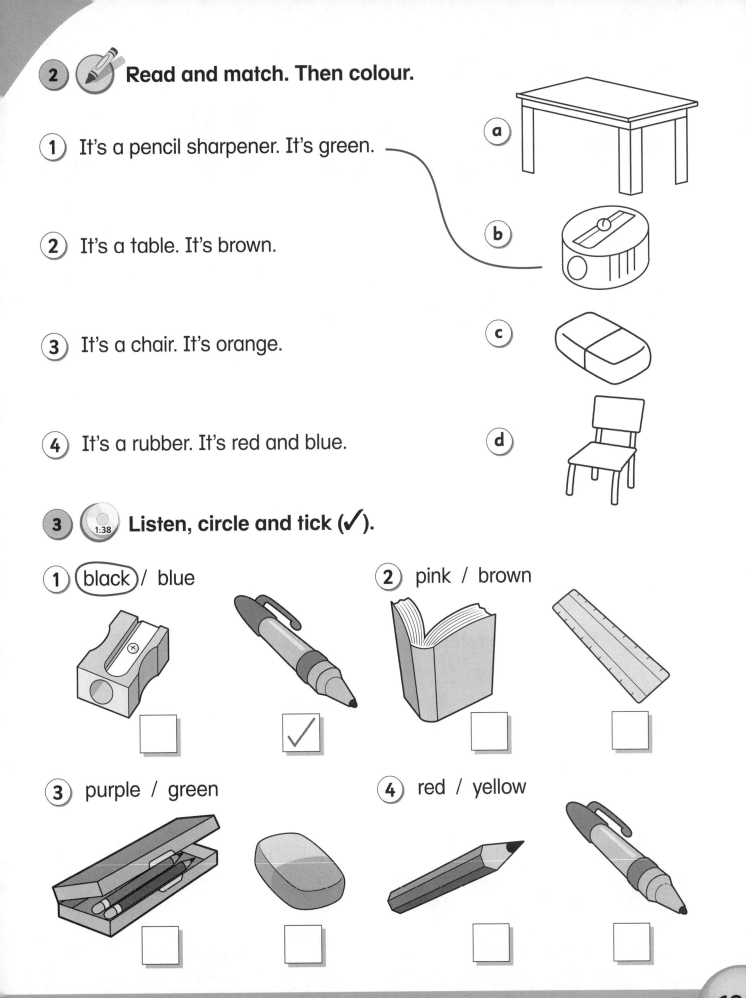

Lesson 2 grammar (*What's this? It's a book. It's red. It's a red book.*)

4 🖊 **Match and trace.**

11 **13** **15** **17** **19**

12 **14** **16** **18** **20**

a sixteen

e fourteen

i nineteen

c eleven

g fifteen

b eighteen

d twenty

f thirteen

h seventeen

j twelve

5 🖊 **Read and circle.**

fifteen pencils.

twelve rulers.

Lesson 3 vocabulary (numbers 11–20)

6 🎧 1:42 **Listen and number. Then colour.**

a

b

c

d

☐   1   ☐   ☐

7 ✏️ **Read and circle. Then tick (✓).**

1 What's this? /
What are (these?)

It's a chair.
They're chairs.

☐
✓

2 What's this? /
What are these?

It's a pen.
They're pens.

☐
☐

3 What's this? /
What are these?

It's a table.
They're tables.

☐
☐

4 What's this? /
What are these?

It's a pencil sharpener.
They're pencil sharpeners.

☐
☐

Lesson 4 grammar (*What are these? They're pencils. What colour are they? They're red.*)

8 🔘 1:43 **Listen and tick (✓).**

STORY

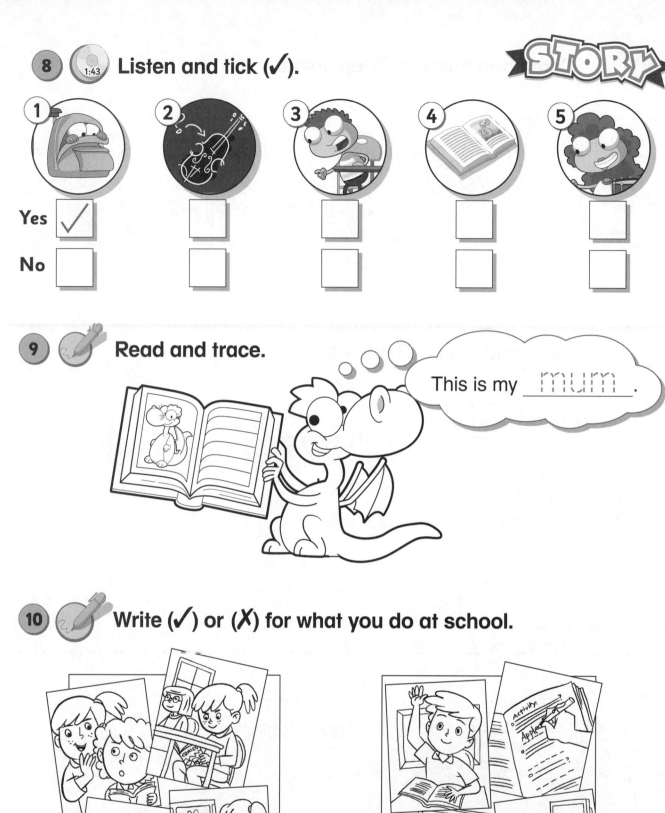

	1	2	3	4	5
Yes	✓				
No					

9 🖊 **Read and trace.**

This is my _mum_.

10 🖊 **Write (✓) or (✗) for what you do at school.**

11 🖊 **Read the words and circle.**

| dip | man | nap | pan |

12 🔊 1:48 **Listen to the sounds and circle the letters.**

1
a (d)
m n

2
d m
i
p

3
a i
n t

4
p
d
i
t

13 🔊 1:49 **Listen and write the letters.**

1 __m__ 2 ____ 3 ____ 4 ____

14 🔊 1:50 **Listen and write the words.**

1 __s i t__ 2 ____ 3 ____ 4 ____

15  Match and trace.

piano   **guitar**   _drum_   _violin_

16  Read and circle.

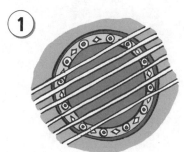
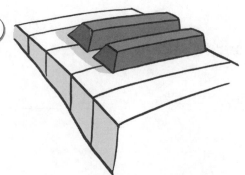
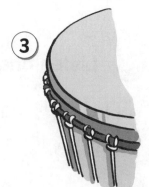

It's a (guitar / drum).   It's a (piano / violin).   It's a (piano / drum).

Wider World

17 Trace and match.

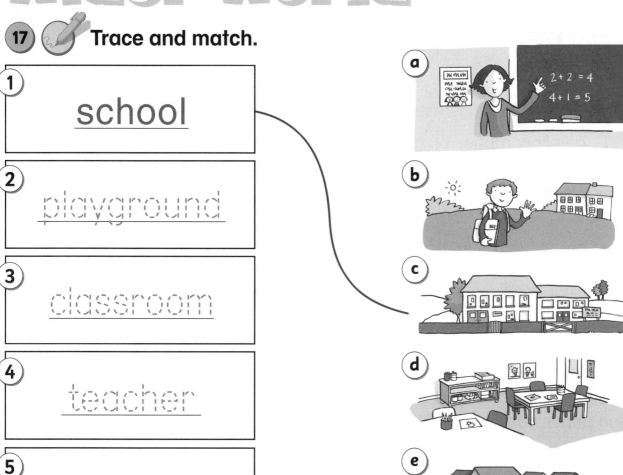

1. school
2. playground
3. classroom
4. teacher
5. pupil

a
b
c
d
e

18  Look at your classroom. Count and write.

1. How many tables can you see? I can see seven tables.

2. How many chairs can you see? _____

3. How many books can you see? _____

4. How many backpacks can you see? _____

5. How many pencil cases can you see? _____

6. What colour is your pencil case? _____

Unit Review

19 **Read and match. Then colour.**

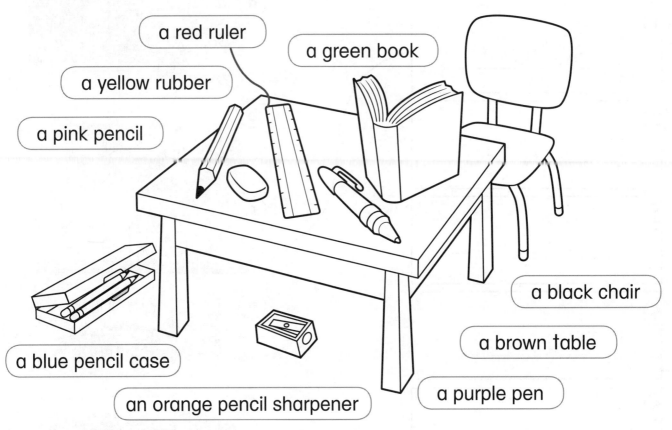

a red ruler

a green book

a yellow rubber

a pink pencil

a black chair

a brown table

a blue pencil case

an orange pencil sharpener

a purple pen

20 **Join the dots. Then read and circle.**

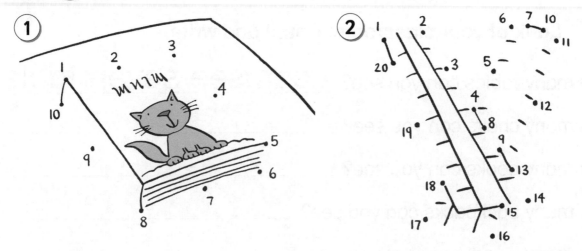

1

2

What's this? / What are these?

It's a book. / They're pencils.

What's this? / What are these?

It's a backpack. / They're rulers.

26

Lesson 9 review and consolidation

About Me

21 Read and circle. Then colour.

¹ ((This) / These) is my desk.

² (This / These) are my books.

They're red and blue.

And ³ (this / these) is my pencil case. It's pink.

Can you see two pens?

They're green.

22 Draw your desk and write.

This is my _____.

These are my _____.
They're _____.

And this is my _____.
It's _____.

Can you see _____?
They're _____.

1 Trace and number.

1. dad   2. mum   3. sister   4. brother

This is my _family_.

5. grandad
6. granny
7. friend

Read and circle. Then find and colour.

This is my (mum / (friend)).

He's ((nine) / ten).

This is my (granny / sister).

She's (seven / eight).

3 **Trace and match.**

seven five ~~eight~~ ten

1   How old is he? He's eight .

2   How old is she? She's seven .

3   How old is she? She's five .

4   How old is he? He's ten .

Lesson 2 grammar (*This is my brother/sister. How old is he/she? He's/She's nine.*)

29

4 **Look and write.**

vet   pilot   doctor   dentist   ~~cook~~   artist   farmer   dancer

a

cook

b

_____

c

_____

d

_____

e

_____

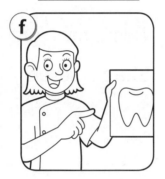
f

_____

g

h

_____

 5 **Read and circle.**

My mum / dad
is a farmer / doctor.

My mum / dad
is a pilot / teacher.

6 **Match. Then read and circle.**

1 Is she a doctor? (Yes, she is.) / No, she isn't.

2 Is she an artist? Yes, she is. / No, she isn't.

3 Is he a vet? Yes, he is. / No, he isn't.

4 Is he a teacher? Yes, he is. / No, he isn't.

7 **Listen and tick (✓). Then write.**    ~~cook~~ doctor artist pilot

1
☐ Yes, he is.
✓ No, he isn't.
He's a ___cook___.

2
☐ Yes, she is.
☐ No, she isn't.
She's a _____.

3
☐ Yes, he is.
☐ No, he isn't.
He's an _____.

4
☐ Yes, she is.
☐ No, she isn't.
She's a _____.

8 ✏️ **Read and find. Then circle.**

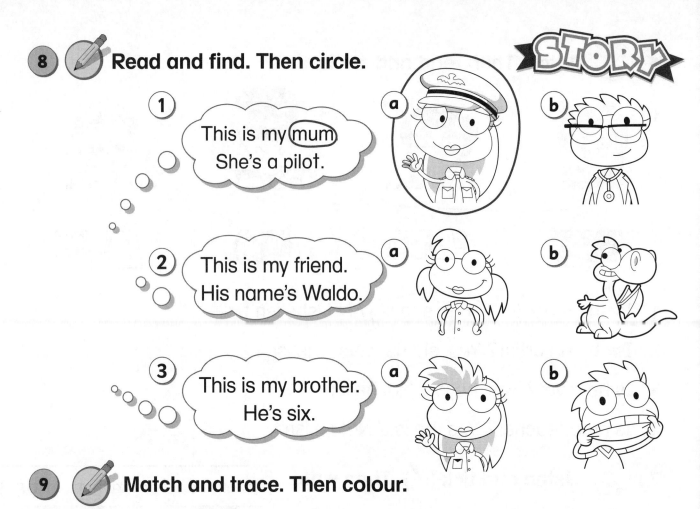

1 This is my (mum)
  She's a pilot.

2 This is my friend.
  His name's Waldo.

3 This is my brother.
  He's six.

9 ✏️ **Match and trace. Then colour.**

1 dad   2 mum   3 granny

4 grandad   5 sister   6 brother

me

Lesson 5 story and values (love your family)

10 Read the words and circle.

can cap dig dog

c g o

11 (1:69) Listen to the sounds and circle the letters.

1 g c o t

2 c o g a

3 i g a p

4 o a c g

12 (1:70) Listen and write the letters.

1 C   2 _____   3 _____

13 (1:71) Listen and write the words.

1 g a s   2 _____   3 _____   4 _____

Lesson 6 phonics (c, g, o)

14 🖌️ **Read and write.**

| drawing   sculpture   ~~painting~~   collage |

1 It's a ___painting___ . ◎▷ **a**

2 It's a _____ . ◎▷ **b**

3 It's a _____ . ◎▷ **c**

4 It's a _____ . ◎▷ **d**

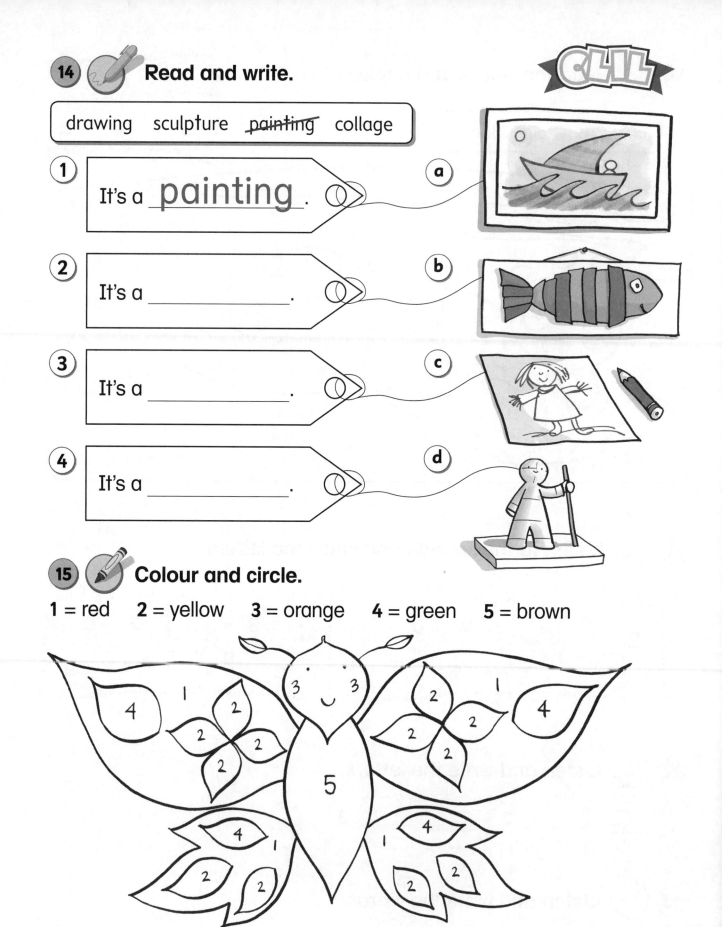

15 ✏️ **Colour and circle.**

1 = red   **2** = yellow   **3** = orange   **4** = green   **5** = brown

It's a painting / collage. It's a bird / butterfly.

Wider World

16 Look and draw. Then listen and number.

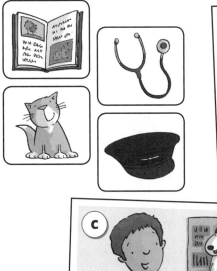

17 Read and answer. Then ask a friend.

Yes, he is.   No, he isn't.   Yes, she is.   No, she isn't.

	me	my friend
Is your dad a farmer?		
Is your mum an artist?		
Is your brother a cook?		
Is your sister a dancer?		

Unit Review

18 🔘 1:77 **Listen. Circle *True* or *False*.**

This is my ~~family~~.

1 (True.) / False.
2 True. / False.
3 True. / False.
4 True. / False.
5 True. / False.

19 ✏️ **Look at Activity 18. Read and circle.**

1 This is my (mum) / dad. She's a vet / (pilot.)

2 This is my dad / grandad. He's a doctor / dentist.

3 This is my sister / brother. His / Her name's Rita.

4 This is my sister / brother. His / Her name's Vava.

5 This is Oscar / Millie. He's / She's my friend.

About Me

20 **Read and write.**

mum ~~dad~~ brother

This is my family. This is my
¹ ___dad___. He's a doctor.
His name's Paul.

My ² _____ is a vet.
Her name's Alice.

And this is my ³ _____.
He's two! His name's Sam.

21  **Draw one person in your family and write.**

This is my _____.

He's / She's a _____.

His / Her name's _____.

4 My body

1 Look and write. Then colour.

head   toes   feet   legs   hands   body   fingers   arms

1 head

2 _____

3 _____

4 _____

5 _____

6 _____

7 _____

8 _____

2  **Read. Then circle.**

1 feet   a    b    c

2 wings   a    b    c

3 tail   a    b    c

4 arms   a    b    c

3 **Listen and circle. Then colour.**

1 I've got a (pink / (purple)) body.

2 I've got (brown / orange) hands.

3 I've got (yellow / blue) feet.

4 **Read and match. Then write and colour.**

| socks   skirt   T-shirt   hat   dress   jumper   trousers   ~~shoes~~ |

1 I've got brown shoes.   **a** 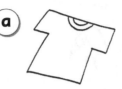 _____

2 I've got a pink hat.   **b**  _____

3 I've got a red dress.   **c**  _____

4 I've got purple socks.   **d**  shoes

5 I've got a green jumper.   **e**  _____

6 I've got black trousers.   **f**  _____

7 I've got a blue skirt.   **g**  _____

8 I've got a grey T-shirt.   **h**  _____

5 Count and write. Then colour.

| six | four | eight | ~~one~~ |

1 She's got **one** head. It's red.

2 She's got _____ arms. They're black.

3 She's got _____ feet. They're blue.

4 She's got _____ toes. They're yellow.

5 She's got a green dress.

  6 Follow. Then choose and write.

1 (He's)/ She's got a ___**hat**___ .

2 He's / She's got a _____ .

3 He's / She's got _____ .

4 He's / She's got _____ .

Lesson 4 grammar (*He's got blue trousers./She's got a yellow head.*)

7 **Listen and colour. Then write.**

| pink   blue   ~~yellow~~   red |

1  **2**  **3**

Millie has got _____yellow_____ hands.

Zak has got _____ feet.

Vava has got _____ feet and a _____ body.

8 **Look and tick (✓).**

9 Read the words and circle.

ck   e   k

~~kick~~   kid   neck   sock

10 2:15 Listen to the sounds and circle the letters.

1
k
e   (i)
a

2
d
t   k
e

3
a
e   k
o

4
a
i   ck
g

11 2:16 Listen and write the letters.

1 <u>k</u>   2 _____   3 _____

12 2:17 Listen and write the words.

1 <u>k i t</u>   2 _____   3 _____   4 _____

13 **Read and circle.**

14 **Listen and check your answers.**

Wider World

15 Carnival masks. Read and match.

1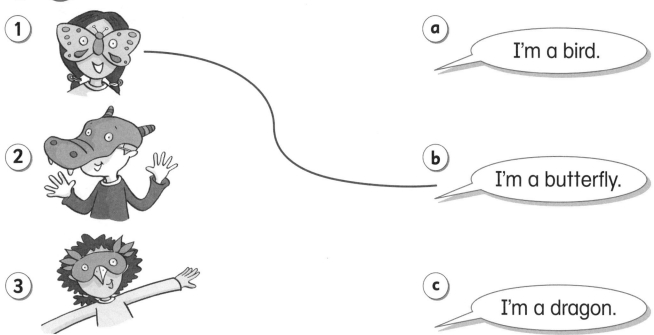

a   I'm a bird.

2

b   I'm a butterfly.

3

c   I'm a dragon.

16 Choose a carnival costume. Colour and write.

a   b   c

This is my carnival costume.

I've got _____ and a _____.

Unit Review

17 🖊 **Read and circle. Then colour.**

1 I've got a (body / (foot)).

   ((It's) / They're) green.

2 I've got three (finger / fingers).

   (It's / They're) pink.

3 I've got five (leg / legs).

   (It's / They're) brown.

4 I've got (feet / foot).

   (It's / They're) orange.

18 **Look and write (✓) or (✗).**

1 He's got a clean T-shirt. ☒

2 She's got a dirty dress. ☐

3 He's got dirty boots. ☐

4 She's got clean shoes. ☐

About Me

19 **Read and write. Then colour.**

arms   eight   ~~head~~   three

This is my monster. He's got
one ¹ <u>head</u> . It's yellow.
He's got a green body.

He's got two ² _____.
They're pink. And he's got
³ _____ purple fingers.

He's got three legs. They're
blue. And he's got
⁴ _____ black feet.

He's got a green hat.
His name's Spike!

20 **Draw a monster and write.**

This is my monster.
He's got one _____.
It's _____.
He's got _____.
They're _____.
He's got_____.
They're _____.
His name's _____!

5 Pets

1 **Look and write.**

frog   cat   dog   hamster   mouse   ~~parrot~~   rabbit   snake   tortoise

1

parrot

2

_____

3

_____

4

_____

5

_____

6

_____

7

_____

8

_____

9

_____

2  **Find and circle.**

1 a snake　　**2** two frogs　　**3** a parrot　　**4** a tortoise　　**5** three mice

3  **Look at Activity 2. Read and circle.**

1 (What's that?) / What are those? (It's a snake.) / They're snakes.

2 What's that? / What are those?　It's a frog. / They're frogs.

3 What's that? / What are those?　It's a parrot. / They're parrots.

4 What's that? / What are those?　It's a tortoise. / They're tortoises.

5 What's that? / What are those?　It's a mouse. / They're mice.

4  **Look and write.**

①    ②    ③    ④

small _____   _____   _____   _____

⑤    ⑥    ⑦    ⑧

_____   _____   _____   _____

5  **Look and write.**

| frog | ~~rabbit~~ | cat | dog |

1 He's got a __rabbit__ .   **3** He's got a _____ .

2 She's got a _____ .   **4** She's got a _____ .

① ② ③ ④

6  **Listen, look and tick (✓).**

1 Yes, he has. [✓]

No, he hasn't. [ ]

2 Yes, she has. [ ]

No, she hasn't. [ ]

3 Yes, he has. [ ]

No, he hasn't. [ ]

4 Yes, she has. [ ]

No, she hasn't. [ ]

5 Yes, he has. [ ]

No, he hasn't. [ ]

6 Yes, she has. [ ]

No, she hasn't. [ ]

7 **Read and circle about your pets.**

1 Have you got a big dog? Yes, I have. / No, I haven't.

2 Have you got a small dog? Yes, I have. / No, I haven't.

3 Have you got a fat cat? Yes, I have. / No, I haven't.

4 Have you got a small rabbit? Yes, I have. / No, I haven't.

5 Have you got an old cat? Yes, I have. / No, I haven't.

51

Lesson 4 grammar (*Have you got a parrot? Yes, I have. / No, I haven't.*)

8 Look and number.

a

b

c

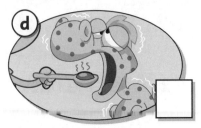
d

e

9 Read and circle.

Waldo is a (dragon) / tortoise. He's got two / three arms and two / three legs. He has / hasn't got wings. He's young / old.

10 Who lives here? Look, match and say.

11 ✏️ **Read the words and circle.**

bag   cup   hat   rat

PHONICS

b   h   r   u

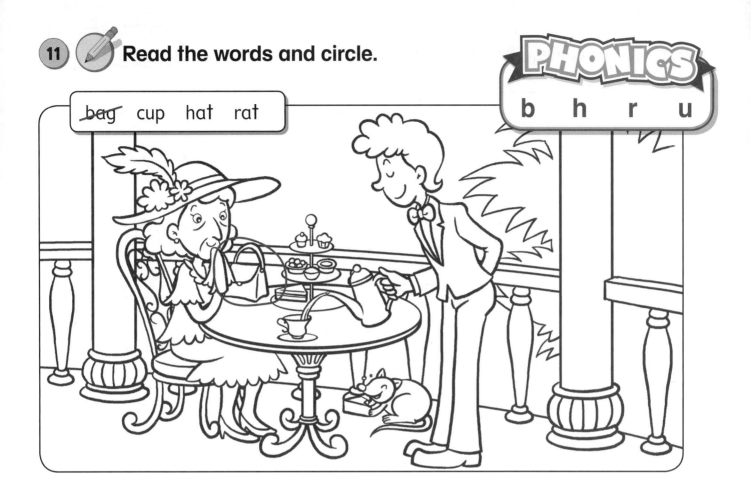

12 💿 2:38 **Listen to the sounds and circle the letters.**

1
n   r
   b
(h)

2
   h
r   u
   b

3
      b
a
   r
   u

4
   n
      h
b
   p

13 💿 2:39 **Listen and write the letters.**

1 __r__   2 _____   3 _____   4 _____

14 💿 2:40 **Listen and write the words.**

1 __u p__   2 _____   3 _____   4 _____

15 **Write. Then match.**

chick   kitten   puppy

1 _____   2 _____   3 _____

16 **Join the dots. Then read and circle.**

It's a (kitten / puppy / chick).   It's a (kitten / puppy / chick).

Wider World

17 Follow and write.

rat tortoise snake ~~spider~~

1 I've got a <u>spider</u>.

a

2 I've got a _____.

b

3 I've got a _____.

c

4 I've got a _____.

d

18 Look at Activity 17. Choose and write.

Yes, I have.   No, I haven't.

Have you got a snake?

Have you got a snake?

1 _____.

2 _____.

19 Read and answer.

1 Have you got an unusual pet? _____

2 What pet have you got? _____

Unit Review

20 **Read and answer.**

| ~~Yes, he has.~~ | No, he hasn't. | Yes, she has. | No, she hasn't. |

1

2

1 Has he got a dog?

Yes, he has .

2 Has she got a rabbit?

_____

3 Has he got a parrot?

_____

4 Has she got a frog?

_____

21 **Read and match. Then write.**

| thin | small | ~~old~~ | long | young | ~~fat~~ |

1 What's that?

It's a dog. It's ___old___ and ___fat___.

2 What are those?

They're snakes. They're _____ and _____.

3 What are those?

They're kittens. They're _____ and _____.

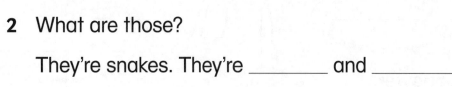
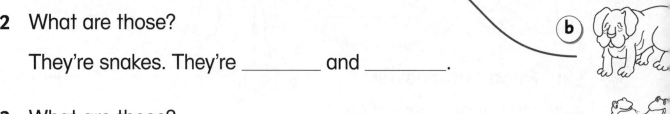

a

b

c

About Me

22 Read and circle. Then colour.

I've got a ¹ (puppy / (kitten)).

He's ² (black / blue) and white.

He's got ³ (two / four) legs.

He's got a ⁴ (long / short) tail.

⁵ (His / Her) name's Minty.

23 Draw a pet and write.

I've got a _____.

He's / She's _____ and

_____.

He's / She's got _____ legs.

He's / She's got a _____ tail.

His / Her name's _____.

6 My house

1 ✏️ **Draw then write.**

bathroom   bedroom   garden   door   kitchen
living room   ~~window~~

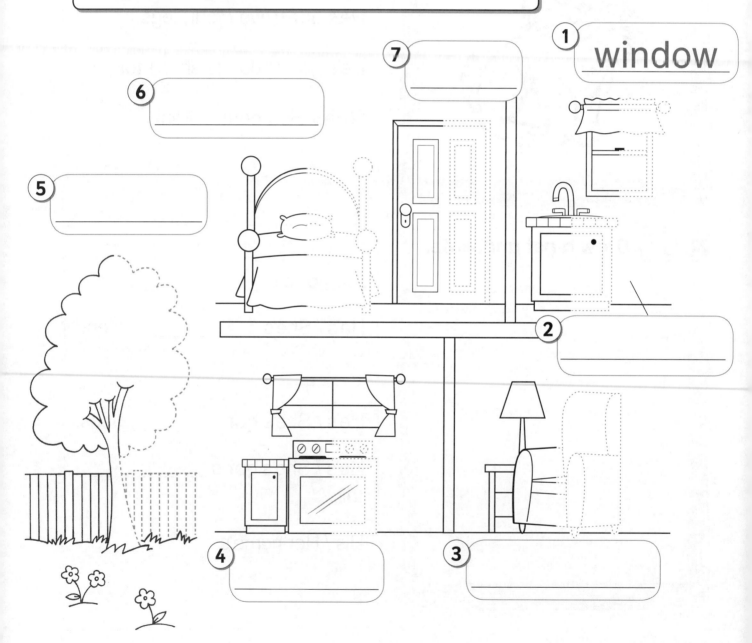

1 window

7

6

5

2

4

3

2 **Listen and number. Then read and match.**

He's in the bathroom.

She's in the bedroom.

She's in the kitchen.

They're in the living room.

3 ✏️ **Join the dots. Then read and circle.**

(Where's / Where are) Waldo?

He's in the (kitchen / living room).

Lesson 2 grammar (*Where's my dad/mum? He's/She's in the living room.*)

4 (2:54) **Listen and number.**

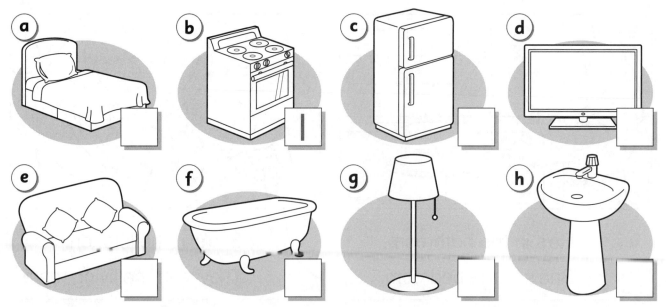

a

b [1]

c

d

e

f

g

h

5 **Look, read, and circle.**

1 They're in the
(bathroom / bedroom).

2 They're in the
(living room / bathroom).

3 They're in the
(garden / kitchen).

6 **Read and find. Then circle and write.**

bed	desk	fridge	sofa	~~table~~	bath

1 Where is the lamp?
The lamp ((is) / are) on the ___table___ .

2 Where are the rabbits?
The rabbits are (on / in) the _____ .

3 Where is the teddy bear?
It is (under / in) the _____ .

4 Where is the boy?
He is (on / in) the _____ .

5 Where are the books?
The books (is / are) on the _____ .

6 Where are the dogs?
The dogs are (on / under) the _____ .

Lesson 4 grammar (*There's a lamp on the desk. There are two kittens on the sofa.*)

7 Look and match. Then write.

| bathroom | kitchen | living room | bedroom |

Dad is in the __living room__. Zak is in the _____.

Rita is in her _____. Vava and Waldo are in the _____.

8 Look and draw.

My bedroom

9 🖊 **Read the words and circle.**

bell   doll   fan   leg

10 (2:61) **Listen to the sounds and circle the letters.**

1
f   s   ff   ll

2
h   o   ff   ll

3
l   h   f   r

4
i   f   t   l

11 (2:62) **Listen and write the letters.**

1 _ll_   2 _____   3 _____   4 _____

12 (2:63) **Listen and write the words.**

1 _f i g_   2 _____   3 _____   4 _____

13 **Write. Then listen and follow the path.**

café ~~house~~ library playground shop

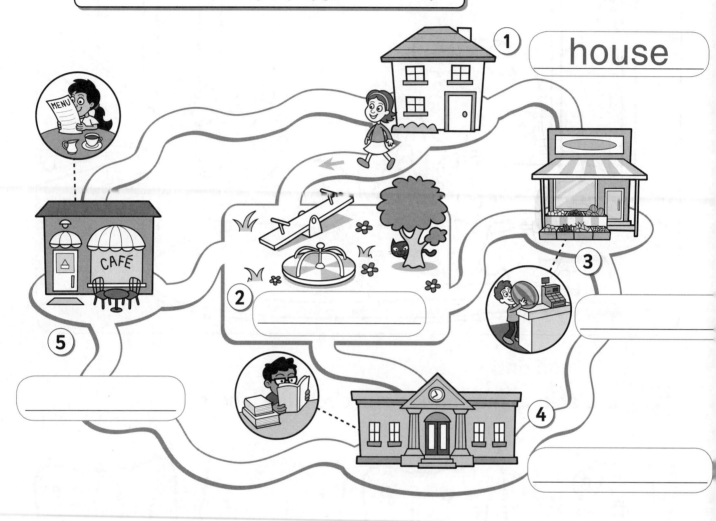

1 house

2 _____

3 _____

4 _____

5 _____

14 **Find and circle.**

1 She's in the
(zoo / café).

2 It's in the
(shop / park).

3 He's in the
(library / café).

Wider World

15 🖊️ **Read and match.**

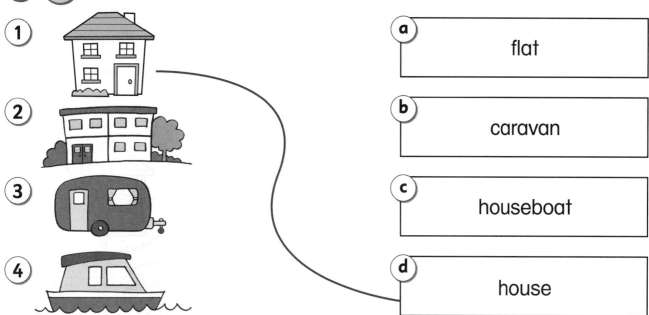

1

2

3

4

a   flat

b   caravan

c   houseboat

d   house

16 🖊️ **Read and complete the letter.**

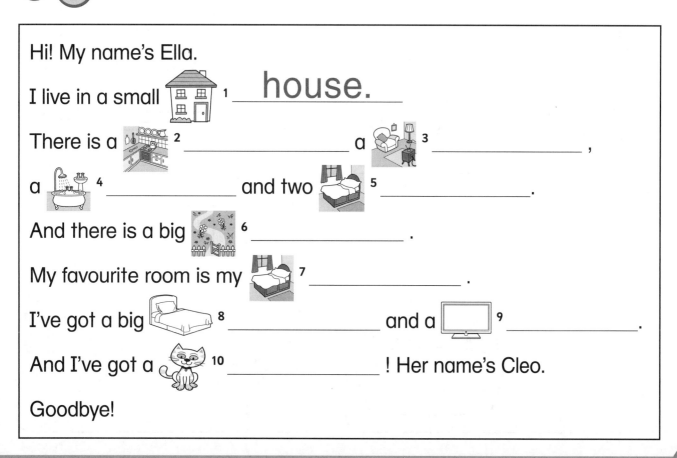

Hi! My name's Ella.

I live in a small [house image] 1 ___house.___

There is a [kitchen image] 2 _____ a [living room image] 3 _____ ,

a [bathroom image] 4 _____ and two [bedroom image] 5 _____ .

And there is a big [garden image] 6 _____ .

My favourite room is my [bedroom image] 7 _____ .

I've got a big [bed image] 8 _____ and a [TV image] 9 _____ .

And I've got a [cat image] 10 _____ ! Her name's Cleo.

Goodbye!

Unit Review

17 2:69 **Listen and draw.**

About Me

18 **Read and write.**

lamp ~~bedroom~~ chairs big two

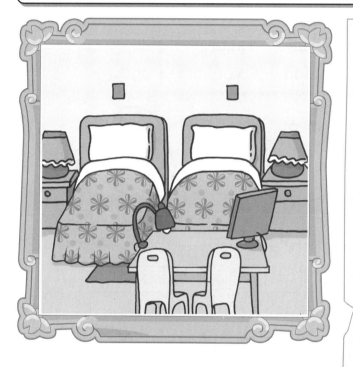

My favourite room is my

¹ __bedroom__ .

It's ² _____ .

There are ³ _____

beds and two ⁴ _____ .

There's a table.

There's a ⁵ _____ on

the table.

I've got a TV.

19 **Draw your favourite room and write.**

My favourite room is my

_____ .

It's _____ .

There is _____ .

There are _____ .

I've got a _____ .

1 🖊 **Draw. Then write.**

bread	cheese	chicken	fruit	juice
~~meat~~	milk	lemonade	salad	yoghurt

1

meat

2

3

4

5

6

7

8

9

10

2 **Find and colour. Then write (✓) or (✗).**

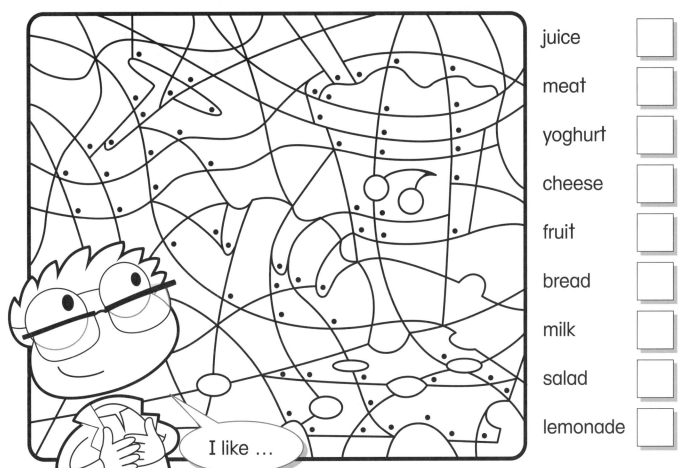

juice ☐

meat ☐

yoghurt ☐

cheese ☐

fruit ☐

bread ☐

milk ☐

salad ☐

lemonade ☐

3 **Read and draw.**

I want meat, salad and cheese.

I want juice.

Lesson 2 grammar (*I like salad and meat. What do you want? I want milk.*)

69

4 🖌 **Look and number.**

honey ☐   ice cream ☐   water | vegetables ☐

jelly ☐   chocolate ☐   sandwich ☐   cake ☐

5 (3:08) **Listen and number. Then circle and write.**

a   b   c   d

☐   ☐   ☐ |

1 I (⟨like⟩ / don't like) <u>honey</u>.

2 I (like / don't like) _____.

3 I (like / don't like) _____.

4 I (like / don't like) _____.

cheese
⟨honey⟩
jelly
meat

6  **Listen and number.**

a [ ]

b [ ]

c [ ]

d [1]

7  **Look and write.**

1 Do you like jelly?

_____ , I _____ .

2 Do you like honey?

_____ , I _____ .

71

Lesson 4 grammar *(Do you like honey? Yes, I do./No, I don't.)*

8 ✏ **Read and match.**

1
2
3
4

a **I like food!**

b **I like fish and fruit.**

c **I don't like fish. I like cakes and milk and ice cream.**

d **I like fish. Do you like fish?**

9 🔘 3:13 **Listen and number.**

a

b   1

c

d

10 ✏️ **Read the words and circle.**

jet   kiss   van   wig

11 🔊 3:17 **Listen to the sounds and circle the letters.**

1
ss   v
c
f

2
w
o   u
v

3
j
v   i
w

4
ss
i   v
j

12 🔊 3:18 **Listen and write the letters.**

1 __W__   2 _____   3 _____   4 _____

13 🔊 3:19 **Listen and write the words.**

1 __m e s s__   2 _____   3 _____   4 _____

14 Follow and write.

1

sausages   chips   carrots

a _____

2

b _____

3

c _____

15 Read and tick (✔). Then draw.

It's good for me!

fruit ☐

salad ☐

cake ☐

bread ☐

yoghurt ☐

milk ☐

juice ☐

chocolate ☐

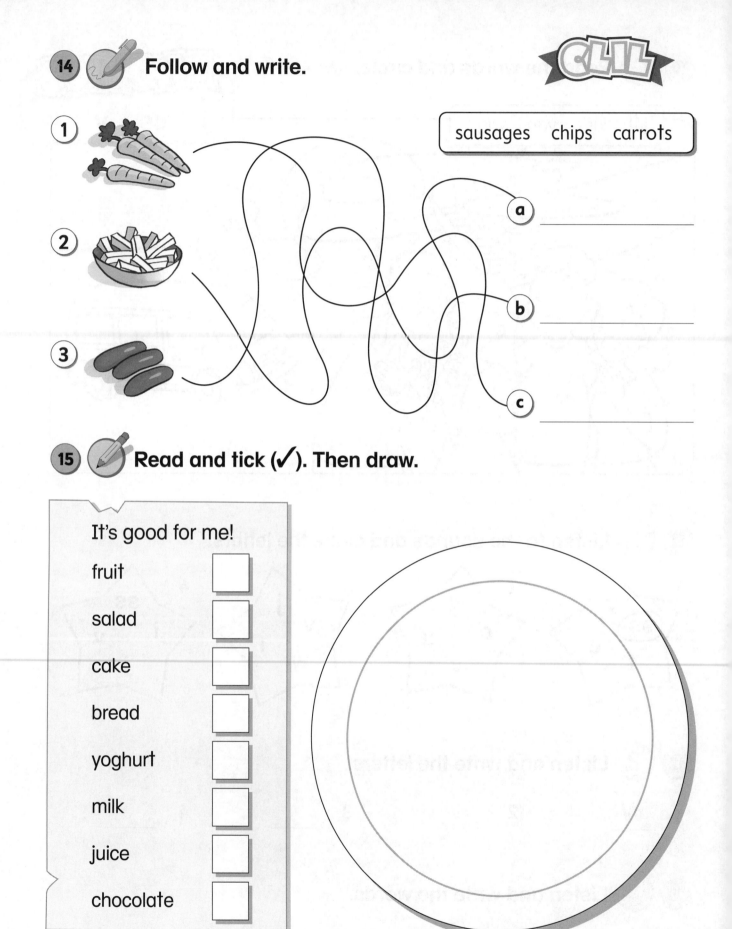

Wider World

16 (3:21) **What does Ella want? Listen and tick (✓).**

Chicken	✓	Rice	☐
Meat	☐	Vegetables	☐
Fish	☐	Salad	☐
Fruit	☐	Water	☐
Ice cream	☐	Juice	☐
Yoghurt	☐	Milk	☐

17 **What do you want? Ask a friend and tick (✓).**

Chicken	☐	Rice	☐
Meat	☐	Vegetables	☐
Fish	☐	Salad	☐
Fruit	☐	Water	☐
Ice cream	☐	Juice	☐
Yoghurt	☐	Milk	☐

Unit Review

18 (3:25) **Listen, draw and match.**

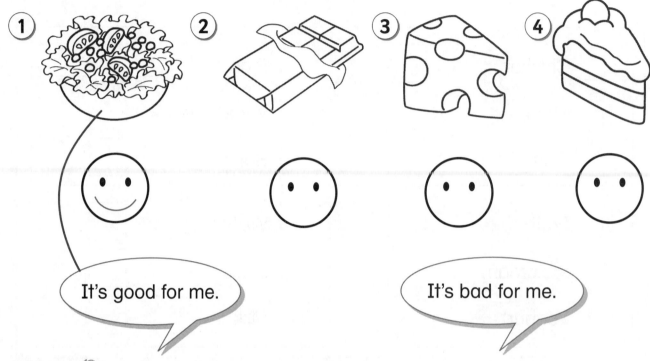

It's good for me.

It's bad for me.

19 **Read. Then choose and write.**

Yes, I do.   No, I don't.

1. Do you like milk?   Yes, I do.

2. Do you like juice?   _____ .

3. Do you like meat?   _____ .

About Me

20 ✏️ **Read and circle.**

I ¹ (like / don't) like chicken and chips.

I ² (like / don't) like fruit.

My favourite food is ³ (pizza / salad).

I ⁴ (like / don't) like sausages.

21 ✏️ **Draw your favourite food and write.**

I like ——————— and

———————————.

I don't like ——————.

My favourite food is

———————————.

8 I'm excited!

1 3:29 **Listen and number. Then write.**

excited   hungry   scared   ~~thirsty~~   tired

a

She's _____.

b

He's _____.

c

She's ___thirsty___. | 1

d

He's _____.

e

He's _____.

2 **Listen and circle.**

1. Yes, I am. (circled)
   No, I'm not.

2. Yes, I am.
   No, I'm not.

3. Yes, I am.
   No, I'm not.

4. Yes, I am.
   No, I'm not.

3 **Find. Then read and circle.**

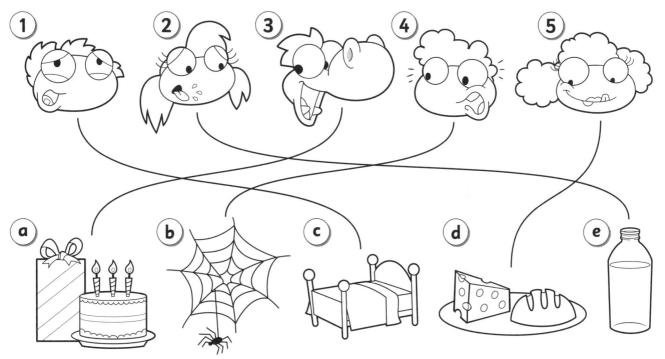

1 ((He's) / She's) (excited / (tired)).

2 (He's / She's) (thirsty / tired).

3 (He's / She's) (excited / thirsty).

4 (He's / She's) (scared / hungry).

5 (He's / She's) (excited / hungry).

79

Lesson 2 grammar (*I'm/He's/She's excited. Are you hungry? Yes, I am./No, I'm not.*)

4 **Look and write.**

| angry | bored | cold | ~~happy~~ | hot | hurt | sad | ill |

① She's __happy__ .

② He's _____ .

③ He's _____ .

④ She's _____ .

⑤ She's _____ .

⑥ He's _____ .

⑦ She's _____ .

⑧ He's _____ .

5 **Read and answer the questions. Then draw yourself.**

Yes, I am.   No, I'm not.

1 Are you happy? _____

2 Are you cold? _____

3 Are you angry? _____

4 Are you excited? _____

5 Are you hungry? _____

6 🔘 3:36 **Listen and number.**

a

b

c  | 1

d

7 ✏️ **Look. Then circle and write.**

1

Are you happy?

Yes, I am. / No, I'm not.

I'm _____ .

2

Are they hot?

Yes, they are. / No, they aren't.

They're _____ .

3

Is she bored?

Yes, she is. / No, she isn't.

She's _____ .

4

Is he tired?

Yes, he is. / No, he isn't.

He's _____ .

8 **Read and circle.**

a He's hot / (excited) / sad.

b He's hungry / thirsty / ill.

c He's tired / scared / angry.

d He's cold / hot / hungry.

e He's happy / excited / scared.

f He's scared / ill / hurt.

g They're happy / hurt / bored.

9 **Look and write.**

1

2

3

Are you _____sad_____? Are you _____? Can I _____ you?

10 ✏️ **Read the words and circle.**

box   buzz   taxi   yes

Yes!

TAXI

11 💿 3:41 **Listen to the sounds and circle the letters.**

1
z   y
x   j

2
x
z   y
zz

3
ck   qu
zz   y

4
w
x   qu
ck

12 💿 3:42 **Listen and write the letters.**

1 ___z___   2 _____   3 _____   4 _____   5 _____

13 💿 3:43 **Listen and write the words.**

1 q u i z   2 _____   3 _____   4 _____

14 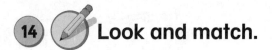 Look and match.

1

It's a long shadow.

2

3

It's a short shadow.

4

15 Read, circle and write.

1

Is it a desk?
Yes, it is. / No, it isn't.
It's a ___chair___ .

2

Is it a hand?
Yes, it is. / No, it isn't.
It's a _____ .

3

Is it a frog?
Yes, it is. / No, it isn't.
It's a _____ .

4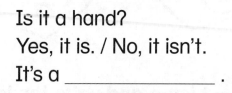

Is it a window?
Yes, it is. / No, it isn't.
It's a _____ .

Wider World

 A puppet show! Listen, read and write.

excited   ~~dragon~~   presents   friends   cake   birthday

1

Hello. My name's Firefly. I'm a __dragon__ .

2 I'm _____ today. It's my birthday.

3 This is my birthday _____. I'm hungry!

4 These are my _____.

5 And these are my _____.

6 Happy _____, Firefly!

Thank you!

Lesson 8 wider world (shadow puppets in different cultures)

85

Unit Review

17 3:48 **Listen and number. Then write.**

a

b

1 She's ___scared___.

2 She's _____.

3 He's _____.

4 They're _____.

5 He's _____.

c

d

e

18 **Look at Activity 17. Read and circle.**

1 Is Millie scared? (Yes, she is. / No, she isn't.)

2 Is Rita sad? (Yes, she is. / No, she isn't.)

3 Is Zak tired? (Yes, he is. / No, he isn't.)

4 Are Waldo and Vava thirsty? (Yes, they are. / No, they aren't.)

5 Is Oscar thirsty? (Yes, he is. / No, he isn't.)

About Me

19 **Read and circle. Then colour.**

This is me on my birthday. I'm

¹ (happy / sad) and ² (bored / excited).

I've got ³ (three / five balloons).

They are red, white and blue.

And I'm ⁴ (hungry / thirsty). I've got

a ⁵ (big / small) chocolate cake!

20  **Draw yourself on your birthday and write.**

This is me on my _____.

I'm _____ and

_____.

I've got _____ balloons.

They're _____.

I'm _____.

I've got a _____

birthday cake!

Goodbye

1 Look and write.

bed   blanket   book   egg   torch   ~~milk~~   mouse   photo   soap

1

milk

2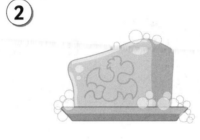

_____

3

_____

4

_____

5

_____

6

_____

7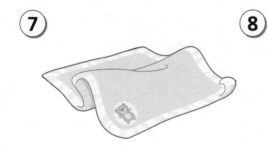

_____

8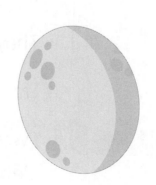

_____

9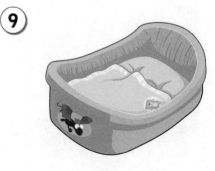

_____

2   **Look, circle and write.**

1 Is it a cat?

((Yes) / No), ___it is___ .

2 Is it a pencil?

(Yes / No), _____ .

3 Is it an egg?

(Yes / No), _____ .

4 Is it a backpack?

(Yes / No), _____ .

5 Is it a blanket?

(Yes / No), _____ .

6 Is it a torch?

(Yes / No), _____ .

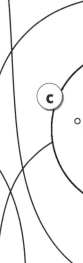

3 3:53 **Listen and number.**

a
b
c

d
e
f ⬚ |

g
h
i

4 **Look and write.**

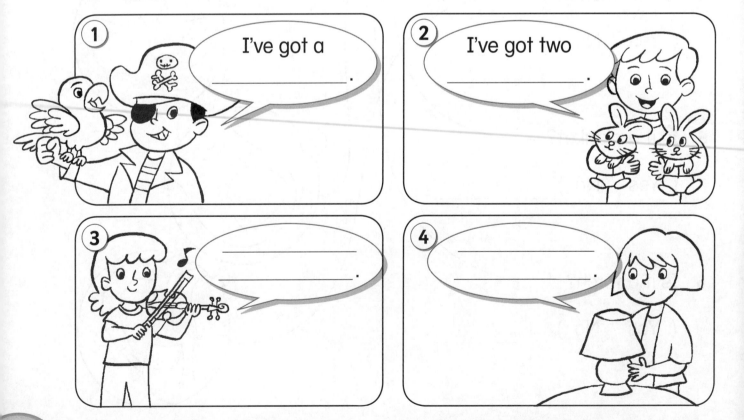

1 I've got a _____ .

2 I've got two _____ .

3 _____ .

4 _____ .

5 Find and circle the odd words out. Then write.

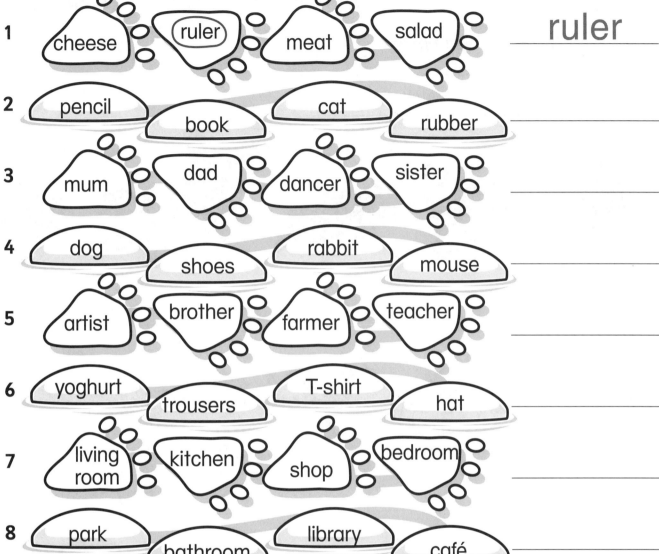

1 cheese (ruler) meat salad   _ruler_

2 pencil book cat rubber   _____

3 mum dad dancer sister   _____

4 dog shoes rabbit mouse   _____

5 artist brother farmer teacher   _____

6 yoghurt trousers T-shirt hat   _____

7 living room kitchen shop bedroom   _____

8 park bathroom library café   _____

6 Read and answer.

1 What's your favourite colour? _____
2 What's your favourite animal? _____
3 What's your favourite food? _____
4 Who's your favourite character? _____

Halloween

1 ✏️ **Match. Then write.**

cat   pumpkin   bat   witch   ~~monster~~

1 ② ③ ④ ⑤

a ⓑ ⓒ ⓓ ⓔ

_____   _____   _____   monster   _____

2 ✏️ **Join the dots. Then circle.**

I'm a monster / pumpkin / witch.

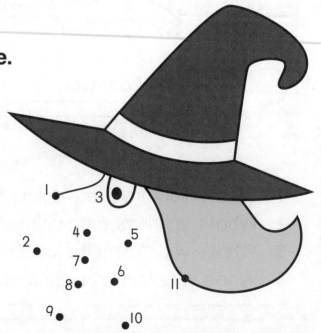

Christmas

1 🔊 3:59 **Trace and match. Then listen and colour.**

a sleigh   **b** present   **c** reindeer   **d** Santa

2 ✏️ **Draw and say. Then read and trace.**

To,

Happy

Christmas!

From Santa.

Easter

1 Colour and write.

| chick   egg   ~~bunny~~ |

 bunny _____ _____

It's an ———————.

2 Look and draw.

1

2

3

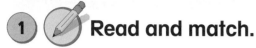

Summer fun

1 🖊 **Read and match.**

a [sun] **b** [sky] **c** [tree]

d [bird] **e** [flower] **f** [grass]

2 🖊 **Choose and write. Then colour the picture in Activity 1.**

[~~blue~~ brown purple yellow green]

The sky is _____blue_____. The sun is _____.

The tree is _____. The bird is _____.

The flowers are _____. The grass is _____.

1 Choose and write.

| My Yes ~~Hello~~ I'm it Her you your is |

a ___Hello___. What's your name?

_____ name's Ellie.

b _____ name's Grace.

c How old are _____?

_____ four.

d What's _____ favourite colour?

My favourite colour _____ blue.

e What colour is your backpack? Is _____ blue?

_____, it is.

1 Choose and write.

| it these ~~this~~ blue pencils They're many they book Three |

a What's
_____ **this** ?

It's a
_____.

b Is _____
red?

No, it isn't. It's blue.
It's a _____
book.

c What are
_____ ?

They're
_____.

d What colour are
_____ ?

_____
purple.

e How _____
pencils can you see?

_____.

3

1 Choose and write.

this   Is   ~~He's~~   She's   my   No   she

a This is my brothor.
_____He's_____ ten.

How old is
_____ ?

b And _____ is
my sister.

c _____ five.

d This is
_____ mum.

_____ she
a dentist?

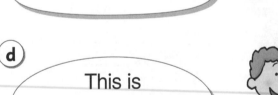

e _____ , she
isn't. She's a vet.

1 **Choose and write.**

| He's | I've | ~~got~~ | They're |

a

He's _____ **got** _____ a blue head and a red body.

b

_____ got four arms. They're green.

c

He's got three legs. _____ blue.

d

_____ got a red head and a green body. I've got blue feet.

5

1 Choose and write.

are   It's   They're   long   you   Has   ~~What's~~   hasn't   I've

a What's that?

_____ a big cat.

b What _____ those?

_____ rats.

c _____ she got a rat?

No, she _____ . She's got a hamster.

d Have _____ got a rat?

No, I haven't. _____ got a snake.

It's a _____ snake!

1 **Choose and write.**

are   Where's   under   There's   She's   They're   ~~Where~~

a

 Where are Mum and Dad?

 _____ in the living room.

b

Where's Grace?

_____ in the bedroom.

c

Hmm. _____ a lamp on the desk. There _____ two rabbits on the bed.

_____ Grace?

d

She's _____ the bed.

7

1 Choose and write.

| please Yes Thank ~~like~~ don't want Do What |

a

I ___like___ sandwiches and fruit. I _____ like chicken.

b

_____ you like chicken, Grace?

_____ , I do. I like chicken. I don't like sandwiches!

c

_____ do you want?

I _____ chicken. What do you want?

d

I want sandwiches, _____ .

Here you are.

e

_____ you!

8

1 Choose and write.

Are   you   they   ~~I'm~~   am   He's   he

a

I'm thirsty.

And ___I'm___ hungry.

b

Are _____ hungry?

Yes, I _____.

c

Is _____ hungry?

No, he isn't.
_____ thirsty.

d

Here you are.

Thank you.

e

_____ they happy?

Yes, _____ are.

103

Picture dictionary

Unit 1

My birthday

red　yellow　green　blue　pink　purple　orange　brown　black　white

Numbers (1)

one　two　three　four　five　six　seven　eight　nine　ten

Actions

jump　walk　stamp　clap　run　dance　climb　hop

CLIL: Science

    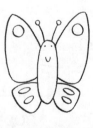

bird　fish　flower　leaf　butterfly

Unit 2

 Classroom objects

chair   table

 pencil

 ruler

 pen

 rubber

 book

 desk

 pencil sharpener

pencil case

 Numbers (2)

 eleven

 twelve   thirteen

 fourteen

 fifteen

 sixteen   seventeen

 eighteen

 nineteen   twenty

 CLIL: Music

 guitar

 piano

 violin

 drum

Unit 3

 My family

mum   dad   brother   sister   friend   granny   grandad

 Occupations

doctor   cook   vet   dentist

pilot   artist   dancer   farmer

 CLIL: Art

 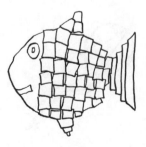  

painting   collage   drawing   sculpture

Unit 4

 My body

head

arms

feet

hands

body

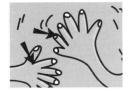
fingers

legs

toes

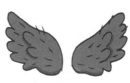
wings

tail

 Clothes

T-shirt

jumper

trousers

dress

skirt

shoes

socks

hat

 CLIL: Science

clean hands

dirty hands

a dirty face

wash your hands

Picture dictionary

107

Unit 5

 Pets

dog

cat

rabbit

parrot

mouse

tortoise

frog

snake

hamster

 Opposites

big

small

tall

short

long

thin

fat

young

old

 CLIL: Science

chick

kitten

puppy

egg

goose

bird

Unit 6

 My house (1)

house

garden

kitchen

living room

bedroom

bathroom

door

window

 My house (2)

bath

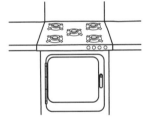
cooker

fridge

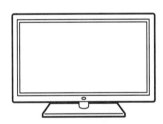
TV

sofa

lamp

bed

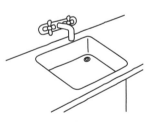
sink

 CLIL: Social Science

shop

library

playground

café

zoo

park

Unit 7

 Food (1)

meat   fruit   bread   cheese   yoghurt

milk   juice   chicken   salad   lemonade

 Food (2)

   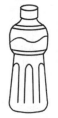      

sandwich   water   chocolate   honey

jelly   vegetables   ice cream   cake

CLIL: Social Science

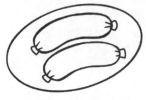      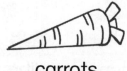

sausages   chips   carrots

Unit 8

 Feelings (1)

| happy | sad | excited | scared | tired | hungry | thirsty |

 Feelings (2)

| hot | cold | ill | hurt | angry | bored |

 CLIL: Science

a long shadow   a short shadow

Pearson Education Limited
Edinburgh Gate
Harlow
Essex CM20 2JE
England
and Associated Companies throughout the world.

www.islands.pearson.com

© Pearson Education Limited 2012

The rights of Susannah Malpas to be identified as author of this work have been asserted by her in accordance with the Copyright, Designs and Patents Act 1988.

Stories by Steve Elsworth and Jim Rose. The rights of Steve Elsworth and Jim Rose to be identified as authors of this work have been asserted by them in accordance with the Copyright, Designs and Patents Act 1988.

Eighth impression 2017
ISBN: 978-1-4082-8988-4

Set in Fiendstar 17/21pt
Printed in Malaysia (CTP-VVP)
GCC/01

Picture Credits
The Publisher would like to thank the following for their kind permission to reproduce their photographs:

(Key: b-bottom; c-centre; l-left; r-right; t-top)

Stickers Page Fotolia.com: Viktor (chicken); Pics721 (house); Matka Wariatka (pencil case); Jose Manuel Gelpi (pencil sharpener); Coprid (desk); Artemisphoto (salad); Anna Kucherova (lemonade). **Shutterstock.com:** V. J. Matthew (garden). **105 Fotolia.com:** Matka_Wariatka (pencil case); Jose Manuel Gelpi (pencil sharpener); Coprid (desk). **109 Fotolia.com:** Pics721 (house). **Shutterstock.com:** V. J. Matthew (garden). **111 Fotolia.com:** Viktor (chicken); Artemisphoto (salad); Anna Kucherova (lemonade)

All other images © Pearson Education Ltd

Every effort has been made to trace the copyright holders and we apologise in advance for any unintentional omissions. We would be pleased to insert the appropriate acknowledgment in any subsequent edition of this publication.

Illustration Acknowledgements
Moreno Chiacchiera (Beehive Illustration), Joelle Dreidemy (Bright Agency), HL Studios, Sue King (Plum Pudding Illustration), Katie McDee, Bill McGuire (Shannon Associates), Jackie Stafford